Sign of the
APOCALYPSE

Sign of the APOCALYPSE

Ruminations and Wit from
an American Roadside
Prophet

John Getchell

Skyhorse Publishing

Skyhorse Publishing books may be purchased in bulk at special discounts for sales promotion, corporate gifts, fund-raising, or educational purposes. Special editions can also be created to specifications. For details, contact the Special Sales Department, Skyhorse Publishing, 307 West 36th Street, 11th Floor, New York, NY 10018 or info@skyhorsepublishing.com.

Skyhorse® and Skyhorse Publishing® are registered trademarks of Skyhorse Publishing, Inc.®, a Delaware corporation.

Visit our website at www.skyhorsepublishing.com.

10 9 8 7 6 5 4 3 2 1

Library of Congress Cataloging-in-Publication Data is available on file.

Cover design by Jane Sheppard
Cover photograph by Cynthia Hall Domine

Print ISBN: 978-1-5107-2694-9
Ebook ISBN: 978-1-5107-2695-6

Printed in China

Special thanks to:
Cynthia Hall Domine
Liz Errico
Ross Kahn
Suzy Campbell

Introduction

"I waited for you, Winterlong, you seem to be where I belong. It's all illusion anyway."

—Neil Sedaka

Winter in Maine can be a grueling affair. Most years the leaves have turned and dropped by the end of October. By the middle of November, the warmth of summer is a wistful memory, and by the darkest day of the year, winter is firmly in residence and has sunk its teeth into the state with the irascible tenacity of a grumpy lobster.

People in Maine find different ways to den down and amuse themselves for the long haul. Random singles couple up for the cold months, ice houses get hauled out onto the frozen lakes, and snow mobiles get readied to molest the general tranquility of the winter woods.

By January, most folks have fallen into a rhythm. The ground is frozen hard, the sidewalks are rolled up, the snow steadily accumulates, storm after storm, not to disappear for months. Most people start the season clearing the snow with resolute, stoic determination; shoveling and plowing and snow-blowing every flake in sight. However, this fervor wanes as the winter storms queue up and unload. By February, there's no place left to put the white stuff, and not much gets cleared other than driveways and narrow foot paths from driveways to kitchen doors. I'm guilty of this.

The winter of 2014 into 2015 was a frigid, relentless beast. By the end of February, the storms had been rolling in at a pace of two or three a week for over a month, and my dogs and I were using a second story window as our front door. I don't happen to be an ice fisherman, I don't own a snowmobile (that runs), and my erstwhile bed-warmer, Trixie Bumbershoot, was giving me chameleon side-eye. Fearing imminent solitude and the onset of cabin fever, I found myself casting about for a new hobby.

Thus begins the strange tale of *The Sign of the Apocalypse*.

* * *

On the fateful day of March 6, 2015, I found myself wandering through the aisles of a cavernous big-box store in south Portland. In the office supply section, I came upon a display featuring a variety of business signage, including an "internally illuminated, portable marquee"—more commonly known as a "letter sign." You know the kind—they sit by the road outside churches and fellowship halls, offering perilous bits of annotated scripture and advertising

You startin' a new church?

upcoming events like bean suppers, bingo nights, and Alcoholics Unanimous meetings. They are usually forlorn affairs. They are designed to be portable and plugged in and lit up at night. Some even come with wheels, but once they get placed in front of a church or the Oddfellows Lodge, they don't do much moving. Rusted and yellowed, their tires go flat, and they slowly melt into the roadside. The signs in front of businesses frequently suffer a similar fate. They become part of the visual cacophony of the landscape along coastal Route 1, tangled by weeds in summer and half covered by the berm from the snow plow in winter, their mobility and capacity for illumination a forgotten promise.

Here is what I had found in office supply. I'm not telling the store's name, nor what it cost.

My first inclination was a simple, obvious thing: find the rest of the letters, write something topically inappropriate, and step back to watch the fireworks. Unfortunately, the rest of the letters were nowhere to be found (someone saw me coming, I imagine), and the available letters didn't show much promise in the impropriety department.

Then, the revelation came to me, a complete and glorious bolt of apocalyptic lightning. This thing, this "internally illuminated, portable marquee," could be mine! I could (and would) set it up directly in front of my house facing the road. I would plug the sucker in—flashing lights and all—and use it to impart

The Internally Illuminated, Portable Marquee.

my observations and words of dubious wisdom to all who passed by! It was sure to amuse and annoy my friends and neighbors in equal measure. A win-win, if ever there was one. My analog Twitter!

I had to pick up the sign at the back of the store—it was bigger than it looked on the shelf.

The lady on the right in the picture asked me whether the sign was for a church or a business. I told her about my plan, the telling of which was growing in length and complexity with each retelling. She listened impassively to my pitch, then rolled her eyes and said, "Looks like someone's got way too much time on his hands."

By the time I got home with the sign, it was getting late in the afternoon. By happy chance, my neighbor, Professor Gallagher, was driving by and saw me trying to wrestle my acquisition out of the back of my pick-up, and he stopped to lend a hand.

I expounded upon my plan, greatly embellished on the hour drive home. The sign would be my one-way sounding board to the world that went past the house. I would be like the town crier (or village idiot, opinions vary) from days of yore, imparting bits of news and words of wit! There would, however, be rules:

- No advertisements
- No proselytization

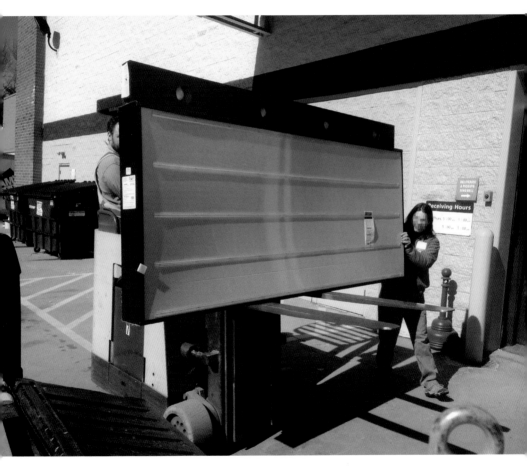

Careful with the baby!

- No overt profanity
- and . . .
- No politics—at least not much!

I also resolved to change the sign religiously on a daily basis until I ran out of things to say, starting on that very day.

Professor Gallagher reckoned that this was perfectly reasonable, and the two of us set about unloading, assembling the components, and installing the sign. Daylight was almost done as we spooled out the extension cord to complete the task at hand.

A passing car stopped, and a woman leaning out the window asked, "You starting a new church here?"

I looked back at my house and tumble down barn and realized that the sign automatically conveyed a connection to the divine upon the humblest of surroundings. Two cars had been forced to brake behind the questioner, and the second in the queue blasted a quick tattoo of impatience.

Me: "Yes ma'am, The Church of the Holy Speed Limit, and this here is The Sign of the Apocalypse!"

Lady: "Well, GOD BLESS!"

Yes! I thought. *The gods bless Our Lady of Irony!*

Luminour in the gloaming.

I don't mind saying I was excited for the following morning to arrive. I had already noticed that traffic on my road was slowing to observe the new roadside curiosity. If you see a cow in a field, you don't think much of it, but a cow on the roof—that'll make you look twice! My mind reeled with possible first posts.

The madness begins: The first sign was a response to the Winter's calling card.

In honor of the promised statewide referendum on the legalization of recreational pasta.

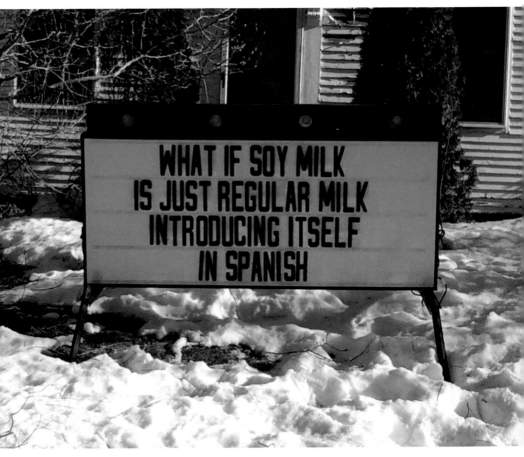

This notion, originally attributed to Bill Murray, was lifted from another sign (that failed to offer any attribution). For all I know, Bill stole it too!

This rule should be observed in the real life—unless read in a mirror.

Sign of the Apocalypse is ideally suited to Haiku format!

Señor Tequila talks me into all kinds of questionable behavior.

This one is the shortest of stories, yet speaks volumes. "Brevity is the soul of wit."

Olde Maine saying!

T. S. Elliot wrote, "I have measured out my life measured with coffee spoons." I say, life is but a series of dogs.

A missive to my tongue.

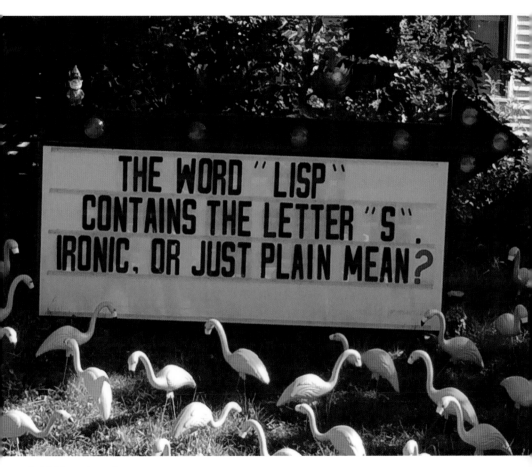

I with I knew the anther.

This one caused some passing cars to pause for longer than usual.

Or perhaps just cold and embarrassed.

Really?

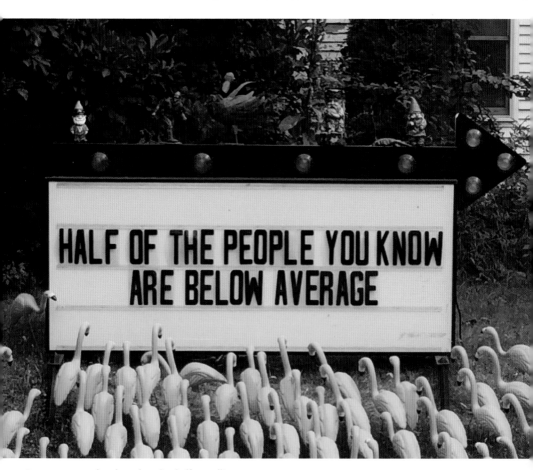

I sometimes wonder about the other half as well!

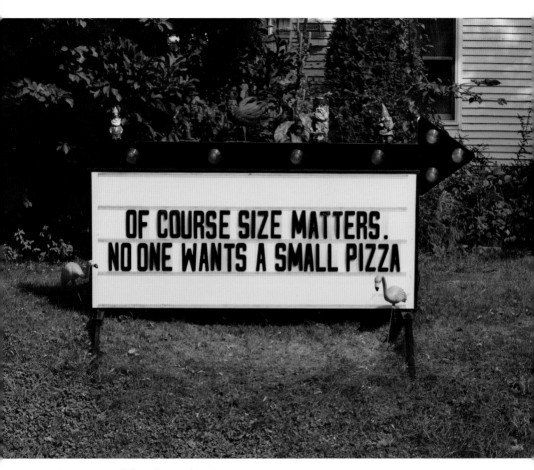

Don't get me started about "personal pan" pizzas!

Unless it is Pink Chablis, in which case it's a crime against grapes.

All hail the oxford comma!

True fact: Men in Maine have a shorter life span than men from away.

I wonder how this one got explained to the kids!

Avocados have fight clubs while you blink.

"Do I look fat?" she asked. Pinocchio paused . . .

Silence is golden. Duct tape is silver.

Excerpted from the *Christmas Elf Handbook*.

There is no Sanity Clause!

Damn ducking straight!

Summer help, some are not.

Or visiting in-laws.

Paltry game hens!

Someone's always watching . . .

Not even to read the sign.

Fifty percent of famous people are below average.

eeting was poorly attended.

Words of wisdom from my doctor.

Bacon and pizza are also compassionate this way.

But breakfast is taken care of!

Wishing the world well, in a sardonic sort of way.

Especially true in relation to pizza.

A good way to thin the herd . . .

And incessant uptalk?

The rest of the week gets a clown suit.

Just one of the charming services I offer.

Surely not EVERYONE was kung fu fighting.

Gin is just a card game.

Funeral home humor always kills!

Another Maine truism.

Oh brother!

Methinks ancient grammarians were sadists.

Boom!

Little known fact: Breakfast foods have body image issues.

Anne hath found her way onto yet another marquee!

Or does the "No-Pants Dance."

Painter's tape is blue and does nothing at all. Masking tape hides nothing.

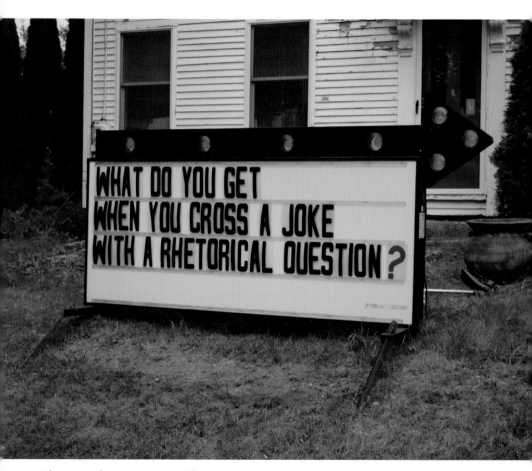

Fifty percent of passing cars stopped for twice as long while pondering this enigma.

Fearing that his pants might combust.

I could ruin this joke by explaining it.

Along with the nectar-thirsty bumble bees.

I should tour the Catskills; I would kill. KILL!

Honest mistake.

T. S. Elliot. Some words of wisdom are without parallel.

Fences don't always make good neighbors.

My kid beat up your honor-roll student.

Cod, that's just painful.

This sign got a lot of "ews!"

A standard kitchen timer in my household.

Total localvore!

I offer a free sizing service.

Fa la la, gobble gobble.

Department of Redundancy Department.

A butterfly flaps its wings in China.

SEAGULLS FLY OVER THE SEA.

IF THEY FLEW OVER THE BAY
THEY WOULD BE BAGELS

Someone should start a Klezmer band called Flock of Bagels.

Stupid avocado fight clubs . . .

The rest of the time it's Scotland.

Said No One Ever was a true sage.

Someone observed that there was a political allegory here. I was offering computer advice.

Also when it's bitterly cold.

When it comes to procrastination, don't even get me started.

No politics, right? Just an aesthetic observation.

I irony in the dryer.

Wrestling with the couch on a daily basis. The couch is winning.

This must be a conspiracy. That's my theory.

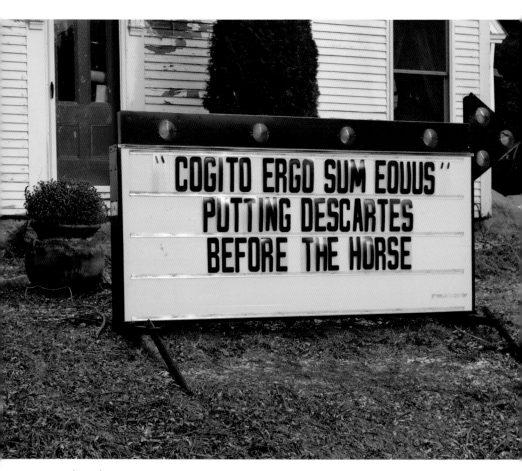

A man has to have priorities.

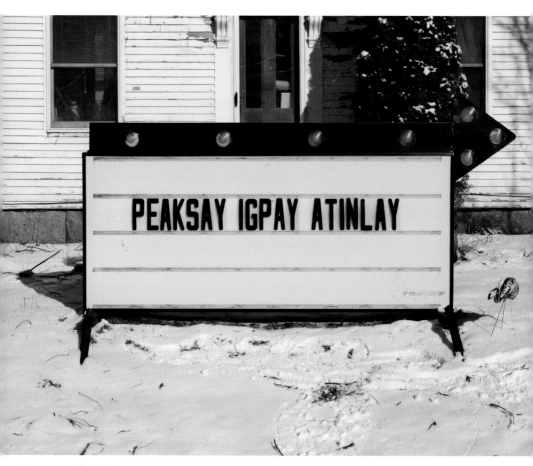

In support of dead languages.

Keeping the tradition alive.

The voice-prompt system didn't get this one . . .

And a toilet that won't close its lid.

And lately at the highest level of government.

Dead of winter blues!

Also, can-can girls.

Words of wisdom.

Or at least last night at 3:00 a.m.

Bigger, too.

Who watched for the moment when the guy wasn't watching the fish.

On my shirt, there is a spottle.

THE DIFFERENCE BETWEEN A WELL DRESSED MAN ON A BI- CYCLE & A POORLY DRESSED MAN ON A UNICYCLE? ATTIRE.

Moral of the story: Stay in your lane.

It this made you happy, you're a meanie!

The fridge is a nosy bugger, too.

SNACCIDENT: N.
EATING ALL THE PIZZA, BACON,
& ICE CREAM BY MISTAKE

Actually, this is an ancient German eclectic emotion

We often end up in a counseling party!

. . . of broken lawnmowers.

. . . at Starbucks.

Apparently, so are a bunch of dragons.

And neither are actually words.

Or the microwave or the fridge.

Hello Mudder, Hello Fadder . . .

The cure: Cialexia?

Unless you're a monkey. Unless you think double.

Paul is dead. Daed si luaP.

Yadda, yadda, yadda—
Whiskey, Rinse, Lather, Repeat.

This sounds like it could be a song!

The sign now has its own sign?

If the bacon is blue, feed it to the dog.

Deja vu, all over again.

"Beer is bread." —Nigella Lawson

Unless you were born a waffle.

And few stop signs.

God, but the line is long here. Have I been here before? Deja vu, all over again.

Maybe I *am* an Internally Illuminated, Portable Marquee!

Conclusion

The seasons traded places in a predictable fashion in that first year of the *Sign of the Apocalypse's* tenure. Before I knew it, I had dutifully posted a new message every day for 365 days, and sometimes—when the spirit moved me—two or three! Much to my surprise, I had neither gotten bored with my postmodern press, nor had I run out of things to say. In fact, the queue of messages in waiting continued to grow; sometimes the product of my own mind and sometimes by contribution from a fan base that continued to grow and take agency in the editorial process.

At one point, it occurred to me that The Sign had ceased to be solely my monster, but had become part of the community—both locally, and as an entity that crackled across the virtual ionosphere—an entity whose reach was growing exponentially from week to week.

I had achieved most of my goals. I had slowed traffic passing by the front of my house (sometimes to a honking crawl), and by all reports, had created a source of snorting amusement for my fellow townsfolk. As the man behind the curtain, I had become a lunatic town crier and The Sign of the Apocalypse, my internally illuminated medium. There were some very happy unintended consequences of the venture. In the summer, the occasional tour bus would take a dogleg down River Road so that tourists could snap pics of the roadside oddity. Also, the four or five school buses that passed by daily would slow so that the pint-sized passengers could take in the daily missive. I then heard that these messages sometimes became a topic of conversation in first period classes, a way to kick off the day, and again around dinner tables about town at the day's end. I also made many new friends, as people would stop to chat if they caught me out in my bathrobe and slippers "changing letters."

I did suffer one ironic disappointment. Every story needs an antihero; every Superman his Lex Luthor, right? The Sign had no detractors! No one with whom to joust! I had carefully prepared my talking points in anticipation of such a challenge, but no dissent ever materialized. Even the good people at Town Hall were fans and turned a blind eye to local regulations governing such signage. The only complaint I have fielded is that sometimes I don't change the sign early enough to suit some people! Sigh . . .

Now we (The Sign and I) are well into the third year of our adventure, with no end in sight. I think there should be a book about it all. Wouldn't that be fun?

Sincerely,
John Getchell